For the Love
of
the Virgin Bride

Donna Gallina

Preparing the Bride

In ancient times, preparation for marriage began when a girl was still very young. A mother had the important job of preparing her daughter to be a good wife and mother as well as preparing her for the coming of the Lord. By virtue and example, a mother would teach her daughter, her princess, how to respect and love her future husband (and children), how to be discreet and chaste, and how to be a homemaker. Learning obedience to her parents was paramount for a daughter in this preparation. The greatest blessing for parents, and their hearts' desire, was to marry off their children and later become grandparents.

In those historic times, it was not only important but also a blessing to begin a family, especially with a son. Sons were preferred because they would stay at home. Mothers love all their children; however, the bond with a daughter was cherished differently because she would bear the grandchildren.

When a Jewish mother gave birth to a baby girl, she would select a special alabaster vessel, or jar, for her as part of her dowry. This jar would later be gifted to the girl for a special use on her wedding night; it could be presented at any time from soon after birth until the time of her betrothal.

The Alabaster Jar

Alabaster is a hard, translucent mineral stone, which is known for its distinctively colored veins; it was often carved into vessels for holding precious oils or ointments. When an alabaster jar was sealed, air and light could not compromise its precious contents.

The alabaster jar, along with its contents, was highly esteemed and was a symbol of purity and great honor. Therefore, it was a very special part of the dowry for a Jewish daughter. This alabaster jar (or box) would hold the blend of fragrant oils the bride would choose for the sacred night of consummation. Every alabaster jar is unique, one of a kind, just as every bride is uniquely special to her groom.

The Fragrance of the Bride

What is the fragrance of the bride? It is a combination of essential oils chosen by the bride. While waiting for her special day, a Jewish daughter, with great anticipation, would carefully and lovingly choose the oils for her alabaster jar. These selected oils would create her special fragrance that would be used to anoint her bridegroom on their night of consummation. The bride would anoint her new husband on the top of his head and the bottoms of his feet in an act of submission.

While growing up, a Jewish daughter would learn about the many oils available, the various aromas of the oils and their particular uses. She learned about the spiritual, emotional and physical significance of each plant and oil. She learned where to buy them, how to mix them, and how to distinguish the pure oils from impure oils. Sometimes the price of an oil would be very high, with some costing as much as a year's wages.

Every time she would hold her alabaster jar, the bride would dream of her wedding night, imagining the sweet-smelling fragrance that would saturate the room that night as she would enter into her covenant of marriage! Her choice would represent her personal and spiritual preference. That night would be one of the most important times of her life and, therefore, she wanted to make this night a night to remember. The fragrance that night would be her own unique fragrance that would become embedded in her husband's memory forever. The most popular and sacred oils chosen were that of frankincense, myrrh, spikenard, cinnamon, and aloes, as revealed in the "Song of Solomon."

Frankincense—Cut from the trunk of the tree and made to bleed, the resin was prized for its many qualities both spiritually and physically. Considered as "the holy anointing oil," it was valued more precious than gold. Uplifting to the spirit, it was given to the priest for use in intercession. This oil was fitting on the wedding night as the covenant was cut and prayers were offered while the bride anointed her husband as the priest and the king of their home.

Myrrh—Highly prized, this oil's fragrance is sweet to smell but bitter to taste. It was often used as a fixing agent in perfume, incense and medicine to make them last. It can elevate feelings, and its sweet fragrance brings a sense of calm. It symbolized the bitter moments of life, but it also imparted a sense of security, knowing that the bond would make the marriage last.

Spikenard—Given the name because of its hairy spikes, spikenard was considered as bestowing honor during the anointing. As a symbol of extraordinary worship, we see the woman in scripture anointing the feet and head of her beloved Jesus.

Cinnamon—Stimulating yet relaxing, it was also thought to attract wealth. The uniqueness of this tree lay in its stiffness and being vertical, expressing the desire to follow the Word of God, to walk straight, and to carry the truth of God's Word in one's heart. Anointing with this oil could bring forth the desire for each other and symbolized inviting God's blessing into the marriage.

Aloes—The tree from which the oil is produced does not yield its fragrance until it reaches at least 30 years. Although the fragrance is light and warming, the arduous process of extracting the sweet-smelling oil is a reminder of the sacrifices needed in a marriage for it to sustain its longevity. The sacrifices made for one another will become apparent throughout the marriage, but it is the passing of time that will bring the measure of sweetness that permeates the marriage.

Preparing for the Covenant

So why is the preparation of the bride so important? Preparation of the bride is important because of the covenant made between the bride and the groom. According to scriptures in the Torah and in the Bible, marriage was the God-ordained relationship between a man and a woman. The preferred meaning of the Old Testament word for "marriage" is "to bond." The marriage covenant is when a man and a woman, in agreement, vow and, having equal benefits and duties, promise to live and work in harmony together until death.

According to ancient Jewish custom, there were two parts to the marriage covenant—the kiddushin and the nisu'in. The first part of the marriage covenant is the kiddushin, or the betrothal. The kiddushin began with a written contract, the bride price, and the cup of wine. "Kiddushin" means consecrated, set apart. It reflects the sacredness of the marital relationship and sets aside the woman to be the wife of one man and no other.

Once the kiddushin is completed, the woman legally becomes the wife of the man. The relationship thus created can be dissolved only by death or divorce. However, the spouses do not yet live together at that time, and the responsibilities agreed upon within the contract do not take effect until the nisu'in is complete.

The second part of the marriage covenant is called the nisu'in; its meaning is "to elevate" and it completes the process of marriage. It is at this point that the husband brings his wife into the chuppah, or bridal chamber, and consummates the marriage through the "blood covenant"; thus, they begin their married life together.

The Man of Her Dreams

Just like most young girls nowadays, a Jewish daughter in ancient times would wait for the man of her dreams. Would he be tall or short, rich or poor, have blue or brown eyes? Where would they meet? In the street, at the well, or maybe even in the fields? Would she be introduced by a friend or arranged by the family? Hopefully, he would be from a good family, hardworking, and secure in wealth and property so as to be a good provider.

Love was not usually the determining factor for the parents who would arrange the marriage; they believed that love would come later. Height and skin color would be considered when choosing a match as those two factors would have bearing on future offspring. Social standing, however, was of the most important aspect when pairing up the two. Affluence and culture would be considered, as compared to ignorance and modesty, and two opposites would rarely be selected for a marriage covenant. Most couples were chosen for political and economic reasons. However, if the child was noncompliant and married beneath his or her status, such individual would be cut off from the family and inheritance.

The Courtship

Courtship did not exist in ancient times as it was customary for marriages to be arranged. Romance was not known, and love was expected to be acquired after the wedding. The idea of "being in love" might have even been considered a mental disease. Usually, the parents of the bride would chose the bridegroom. Sometimes, a wife was chosen at the request of the suitor or the father of the groom. Another option was to employ the services of a matchmaker called a "shadchan." The shadchan could be a professional matchmaker, a friend, a relative, or even a rabbi, and he could require part of the dowry as payment for his service.

Regardless of who arranged a marriage, it was important that the future spouse be from the same tribe or community, but it was even more important that the spouse be Jewish, because this would serve as a way to insure that idol worship or other non-Jewish beliefs would not be influencing the young couple and possibly turn them away from God Jehovah. In fact, marrying someone outside the Jewish faith was not considered a legal covenant. This requirement was significant because a marriage was actually a covenant not just between a man and woman, but between two families.

The traditions of the Jewish community were sacred unto God and were to be kept and handed down from generation to generation. Marriage is a divine institution created by God to sanctify a couple as "holy," or set apart, and from this concept comes the term "holy matrimony." The require-ment of marrying only within the Jewish belief system was also a way to ensure that the nation's future generations would carry on the blessing as well as the representation and the laws of God.

Once the spouses were chosen and agreed upon, the father of the groom would negotiate with the father of the bride. If there was no father, the brothers of the bride or other next of kin would step in as negotiator. Once the terms of the marriage were approved by both parties and the bride, the contract would be written up.

The Bride Price

In early ancient times, the woman was considered an object of ownership as she would first belong to her father and later to her husband. Although considered an object, Jewish women would nonetheless be given great respect and held in high esteem, as evidenced in the scriptures by the woman written about in "Proverbs." However, over the course of time, the status of women slowly changed, and they were eventually given equal standing with men.

The agreed upon payment for a bride was in effect compensation to the bride's family for the loss of the daughter's labor. This payment was called the mohar. The mohar was not regarded as a wedding gift but was sometimes given back to the bride. Every prospective groom was obligated to present the price for the bride, which could be paid with jewels, money, land, labor, or animals. Actually, this bride price would be paid by the father of the groom to the father of the bride. If the father wanted to discourage the groom, he would set an extraordinarily high price for the bride.

Separate from and in addition to the mohar, the groom would give his bride a wedding gift, and that gift was called the matton.

The typical age of the bride at consummation would be the expected age of puberty, i.e., the expected age of child-bearing ability. It was very important that the bride be a virgin on the night of consum-mation, the completion of a marriage covenant as sealed by sexual intercourse. If, however, the bride was not a virgin, the bride-groom had the right of refusal and could demand that his payment be returned.

The dowry was the gift given to the bride for her wedding by her father. If the girl was given a large dowry, it could attract a man of status. Sometimes, the attraction to the bride was just because of the dowry. This was frowned upon and would be considered shameful. The dowry could consist of maids or slaves, valued possessions, house, utensils, furniture, or even land. The father was obligated to provide her wedding gown. A man would seldom marry a girl without a dowry; she had to be of some value to him.

The Signing of the Contract

After the terms of the marriage were agreed upon, a contract called the ketubah would be written up. The ketubah (its actual meaning is "written") was a legally binding document, often a beautiful work of calligraphy; it was considered a keepsake and would be displayed in the home as a reminder of their vows to one another.

The purpose of the ketubah was to summarize the vows and to describe the responsibilities of the bride and groom as they entered into marriage not only with each other but also by the Spirit of God. It would detail the husband's obligations to the wife during marriage, the conditions of inheritance upon his death, and the obligations regarding the support of children of the marriage. It also could provide for the wife's support in the event of divorce.

The betrothal was so binding that the couple would need a written letter of divorce to dissolve the marriage. However, the option of divorce was available only to the husband. The wife would have no say, whereas the husband could request a divorce at any time. Wives often adorned themselves with gold and silver jewelry as well as coins because when a divorce was final, depending on the terms, she was entitled to keep only whatever she was wearing at the time.

After the marriage contract was written up, the prospective groom would go to the home of the prospective bride. He would bring with him the contract, or ketubah, along with a flask, or vessel of wine, and the bride price. At the table, he would present his offering. At this point, the woman had the right to accept or reject the offer. The Talmud, a Jewish law reference manual, specifies that a woman can be acquired only with her consent and not without it.

If the bride agreed to marry the man who presented the contract and agreed to the terms of the contract, she would then sign the ketubah in the presence of two witnesses, and the mohar, or the bride price, would be paid. A blessing would be said over the wine, and the prospective bride and groom would both drink from the cup of wine. Until the time of consummation, they would not drink again of the cup.

The groom would, at this time, give her the gifts he had chosen for her, called the matton, or wedding gift. This gift was to indicate his love for her. It would also be a token for her to remember that he was thinking of her and that he would return for her, as they were not to see each other again until the time that he would come back for her. The groom would then place a ring on the right index finger of his new bride. The ring placed there would be his sign of authority. This ring could not be borrowed, and it must be given to the wife irrevocably. The ring usually was made of silver, which carried the meaning of "redemption." This symbolic act was the final seal and indicated that the contract was now binding. At this point, she truly belonged to him. She was his betrothed.

A celebration would be enjoyed by the family on this day and word would spread throughout the village that there would be a wedding to prepare for.

The Veil

After the contract was signed, the bride would now veil her face in public, and the veil was to be removed only by her husband on the night of her wedding. It symbolized her separation or being "off limits" to other men; it was a symbolic representation of the hymen. The hymen, otherwise known as the veil, is a membrane around the girl's vagina indicating virginity that is to be broken only during sexual intercourse on the night of consummation, thus lifting the bride's veil.

The blood covenant is sacred and treasured in the eyes of God; it is not to be taken lightly. Virginity is a state of the spirit, soul and body; it symbolizes being in a place of innocence that is sacred, undefiled, pure and whole. It is the private, secret place, where all is to be given, but only in the realm of marriage.

The man, as in Adam, was given a wife as his helpmate in order that he not be alone. The helpmate within a marriage was designed to help fulfill the plans and purposes the couple was created for. The beauty of this relationship was also to procreate and to carry on that love and the purpose shared by the marriage partners.

A loving family is the result of a marriage that begins out of a close intimate, committed relationship. The giving of oneself in the sexual relationship, within the confines of this covenant, is not only for the physical pleasure but also to satisfy the spiritual and emotional desire that connects, or bonds, the man and the woman together. It is a covenant made by the shedding of blood.

It is important to understand what a marriage covenant is and to know the dynamic of the marriage blood covenant that can only be made between a man and a woman. A blood covenant in marriage is a solemn mutual agreement and bond between husband and wife, imparting all they are or have to possess in this life, to be available to each upon demand. This covenant is to be broken only by death. The cutting or shedding or mingling of blood would be the most significant part in the blood covenant in marriage.

The Preparation Begins

After the signing of the ketubah and the subsequent acts of traditional symbolism, the groom would now leave the bride to make the preparation at his father's house for the nisu'in (to enter into the covenant of marriage).

The betrothal was a time of preparation for both the bride and the groom. It was not only a time to prepare by gathering things for the comforts of life, but also a time to prepare oneself spiritually, emotionally and physically. For the groom, at the father's house, an addition or a tent would be added to the residence for the new family to reside. The bridal chamber, the chuppah, would be adorned with white linen, gold and purple for the wedding night. The groom's best friend would help with the arrangements for the wedding, as it was the responsibility of the groom and his parents to provide for the celebration of the marriage.

This chuppah preparation would usually take about a year and would provide a time for reflection and spiritual preparation for both the groom and the bride. During this time, there would be no sexual relations. It was essential for the groom to become grounded in the Torah and to seek God for wisdom and direction for his future wife and children. This time of separation was especially important for the groom and the bride as a means to learn patience and dependence on God in preparation for when the difficult times would come. It would also be a time of testing, for some could not endure and would be tempted away from their commitment.

Although legally married, the bride would continue to reside at her parents' house. At certain times, the bride would be allowed to see her betrothed, but she could do so only with permission, only at the bride's home, and only with a chaperone. While apart from the groom, the bride would be preparing for her new life with her husband. The things she treasured and the things she would need were to be gathered and stored in her trunk until her departing day. Her wardrobe would be sewn and prepared; it would include the white and blue linen garment she would wear on the day her betrothed would come for her. The white represented purity; the blue indicated that she would now be royalty. Likewise, her groom's attire would also be in white linen.

The bride's preparations would also include beauty treatments with ointments and oils as she wanted to be perfect without wrinkles or blemish. Her mother would be helping the bride and would reinforce what she had taught her daughter over the years.

Once the groom had completed the chuppah, the father of the groom would determine the day his son was to bring his bride home. Weddings would usually take place in the spring after the winter and the rains, when the flowers would be in bloom. It could also take place in the fall after the harvest. When the groom's father would give his okay, the groom would send his friends before him to tell his bride that the day was soon approaching. The bride would then gather her maids for the mikva. The mikva is a ritual cleansing where the bride is washed in water and perfumed symbolically to sanctify her and cleanse her spiritually of any impurities.

The betrothed would customarily come for his bride at night and in secret, suddenly, and unannounced. To be gracious to his bride, the groom's friends would warn the bride with shouts as they approached, indicating that it was time for her to get ready. The wise bride would have ready all that she needed to bring into her new home, even at a moment's notice. With her maids helping her, she would be bathed and perfumed. With excitement and antici-pation, they would braid her hair and adorn it with garlands of ribbon and flowers such as roses or lilies or even blossoms of myrtle. In ancient times, it was believed that the sweet aroma of oils of flowers and spices would ward off evil spirits. The bride would be adorned with ornaments of gold and silver and jewels. The last and finishing touch would be to dress the virgin bride in her beautiful wedding garment.

While his daughter was getting ready, the father would prepare for the celebration that was about to begin. He would say the wedding blessing over his daughter before the procession began. When hearing the shouts of the groom's friends and seeing the flames of fire from their torches in the night as they approached her home, the bride knew her betrothed would soon be there. There was no time to lose; in an instant, she would be carried away to meet her husband, her lord. The bride and her virgin maids would gather their lamps, the oil and her things. Of course, the one item she would be sure to take was her alabaster jar that held her own special fragrance.

Once the friends of the bridegroom arrived at her house, they would carry the bride out, followed closely by her maids. On a platform fit for a queen, they would carry her to fulfill her dream.

As the procession of the bride went forth in the night through the village, shouts could be heard. In the dark of night, even with the light of the torches, the heavily veiled bride would not be known.

The "Song of Solomon" tells of the groom's military escort; with swords at their sides, they would bring the Shulamite back with shouts of celebration, and the ten virgins by her side, with their torches to light the way. Likewise, the groom's men would bring his bride to him. The "best man" would lead the way, carrying a myrtle branch. The myrtle is a tall, fragrant tree; it has also been known as a symbol of the covering, the Lord's protection. The significance of this practice could have been that the tree represented the material that the booths were made of for the feast of tabernacles.

Soon the bride would come to meet her bridegroom and arrive at the bridal chamber to be carried over the threshold into the chuppah, where the nisu'in would begin. Her most precious gift that she would not be without was her alabaster jar.

And the Two Shall Become One

The day arrived when the father would send forth his son to bring his betrothed home. In the bridal chamber, the chuppah, the two became one, and the bride would now be complete.

The bridal chamber was kept in strict privacy but would be prepared and readied, filled with food and drink and gifts for the bride. It was upon entering the chuppah, that the groom would carry his bride over the threshold. It was then that the authority over the bride was passed on from her father to her groom. It was the first time they would see each other as no one else would have seen them. As they prepared for that night, they began with prayer and would drink from the cup of wine in celebration, and that is when the bride would bring forth her alabaster jar.

The Anointing of the Groom

As the groom reclined in his chair, the bride would bow and drop to her knees. In an act of submission and love, she would break open her alabaster jar, would anoint his feet with the fragrant oil and then wipe them with her hair. The fragrance that filled the air that night would be etched in their minds, along with their love for each other, forever. It would be because of this fragrance and this night that when they would go into public, no other fragrance would tempt them because the memory along with the fragrance of that night would not let them forget. The anointing also represented the Glory of God that was a part of their covenant and that would seal this sacred night in their hearts, minds and souls forever.

The Uncovering of the Veil and the Blood Covenant —The Nisu'in

In this very private and sacred time, as she arose from her knees and stood before her betrothed, he would take the veil from her face and exposed her true beauty. As a priceless gift so precious and pure, he understood the significance of having the honor to come into covenant with his virgin bride. The one he longed for, the one who was now his wife, whom he would hold and caress so tenderly. As they consummated their marriage, the blood was shed, the covenant was sealed that night in their bed, in the chuppah, under the covering and under the anointing.

That night she gave her husband the gift of herself that she had waited so long to give. Spiritually, emotionally and physically, they were joined as one. That night, the virgin would enter into covenant. No one else had and no one else ever would have this moment. Because she had saved herself for him, and he had saved himself for her, in the beauty of that night, together they became one. It was a beautiful night, a sacred night, and in that night, their dreams were fulfilled.

The blood that was shed forth during the time of consummation was a sign of a pure and undefiled covenant. The blessings of this marriage and forthcoming offspring would be produced in faith and in pure, undefiled love for God and for each other. The incorruptible seeds of his love were now sown into the beauty of his bride.

The Celebration

Now fitted together in the eyes of God, when the nisu'in was complete, they would emerge from the bridal chamber adorned in festive attire, and crowns would now be placed on their heads. The groom, surrounded by his friends, and the bride, surrounded by her friends, would greet everyone and all began to celebrate this blessed union. The bride and groom would be carried on a platform with magnificent chairs to be celebrated as king and queen. From here, they would oversee the celebration that would last for seven days.

This celebration was called "the seven days of the feast." It was a time when relatives and friends, and sometimes the whole village, would meet and rejoice with the happy couple. There would be endless food, and wine would flow from large vessels. Raisins, apples and nuts would be staples at the festivities, symbolizing that the couple be blessed with a life that is sweet and fruitful. Nuts would also be scattered before the couple as a symbol for a good and wholesome marriage.

At the feast, friends and family would celebrate with music and dancing as well as playing games and solving riddles. Believed to have been written by a bride and groom, the "Song of Solomon" was sung during this time, and the fragrance of aromatic oils, spices and flowers would fill the air.

The Happily Ever After

Filled with hopes and visions of a growing family, the husband and wife would now begin their new life together. What had begun as a dream many, many years before in a young girl's heart, was now being fulfilled. Her foundation was the love, the mystery, the passion and the beauty of the covenant which was ordained by God. With her husband at her side, she now looked to her future of "happily ever after." After the celebration, they would enjoy a year together before embarking on their official duties as husband and wife. In their hearts, they knew that they would now be the next generation to bring forth and pass on their love for God, for each other, and for their family – to live their "happily ever after."

Restoring the Bride of Christ

Today, we see so many of these Jewish practices lost, and even reversed, especially the beauty of the virgin. The wait and virgin ideal are virtually nonexistent and have come to a place of shame and persecution. The two ceremonies have been combined into one. The selection of the couple has been replaced with "being in love" and often is without commitment. The meaning of the covenant being kept has vanished from society. The standing of the bride and bridegroom has been devalued. God is just a byword and, often, He is left out of the ceremony.

Even in the Jewish community, the betrothal, the wedding and the chuppah are combined into one service. Many of the traditions have been substituted. The symbol of the chuppah is now a makeshift canopy, or the groom covering the bride with a veil, or they are both under the prayer shawl. In these modern times, entering the synagogue or the church has replaced the entering into the chuppah. Not seeing the bride for a year has been replaced by not seeing the bride on the day of her wedding. To rekindle this idea of the virgin back into society would be a great honor. What a beautiful way to restore these practices not only to honor the covenant of marriage and bless the children to come, but also to honor the covenant made before God.

So what do we do if we already have made the error of a premarital sexual relationship?

We have come a long way since ancient times, and we have lost so much. Some girls may not have had the mother or role model to teach them to be like the woman that the Bible speaks of in "Titus," being taught in the ways of God and being prepared for their future husband. They may not have known how sacred the covenant was, did not wait and gave of themselves before the proper time. Some may have given themselves to the wrong man or maybe even to many. Today, fathers have neglected to bring up their sons to understand the sanctity of the marriage covenant and the love for the bride. Society has propagated lust instead of love and has perverted the covenant and the marriage bed. Commit-ment has been replaced by indifference, and honoring God has been left out completely. Consequently, because of these decisions, many people have found out that by not following the plan of God, to their chagrin, their "happy" has turned into "sad."

BUT... GOD can turn that "sad" back into "glad" because God is a God of restoration. We have a redeemer kinsman, and His name is Jesus. He can make all things new! Our repenting and turning makes us pure again. God even invites us to do so. In Isaiah, He tells us, "Come now, and let us reason together, sayeth the LORD: though your sins be as scarlet, they shall be white as snow." Together with God, we are made whole again. Restored, we can now start anew. We can now look forward to the day on earth when we make a new covenant with the man or woman of our dreams.

Are You Willing to Wait?

Whatever the age, almost every single girl is waiting for her bridegroom, and almost every single boy is waiting for his bride. Nearly every girl has visions of her wedding day and the man of her dreams. From her gown to her maids, from her venue to her honeymoon, everything has been sketched meticulously in her mind. Nearly every boy will have visions of how his bride will make him happy, and how he will make her happy. They both have so much to offer, but their desire for love makes it hard to wait.

The temptation not to wait will be great, but there is something special, something sacred, and something beautiful about waiting for love to awaken. Without guilt or shame, pressure, or haste, the two becoming one under the sacrament of marriage is love in its purest form spiritually, physically, and emotionally. Maybe that is why ancient brides were separated from their betrothed until the wedding day.

In today's society, the roles of the virgin bride and motherhood have been lost. The bride to be has been seduced into a false sense of love and has devalued herself to nothing. She no longer sees her value, believes she has none, or believes she would not be worth waiting for. She has been seduced into having sex outside of marriage and has come to believe the only way to have and keep the man of her dreams is to give in to his desires, no matter what they may be, rather than to test his love for her. Commitment to her has become virtually nonexistent. Exposure to porno-graphy, drugs and alcohol are all channels that satisfy the lust of the flesh and misrepresent the marriage bed. The lack of commitment deprives couples of this sacred rite of covenant and defiles the marriage bed. It ruins many a relationship because its desires are never fulfilled. It makes for corruptible seeds that can turn into hatred. In its path of destruction, it leaves rejection, anger, and heartbreak and many times a generation of godless orphans. Love is not meant to be awaken before its time.

God has plans for your future and a promise. "For I know the thoughts that I think toward you, sayeth the Lord, thoughts of peace, and not of evil, to give you an expected end. Then shall ye call upon Me, and ye shall go and pray unto Me, and I will hearken unto you. And ye shall seek Me, and find Me, when ye shall search for Me with all your heart." If you have a heart for God, you will meet the bride or the bridegroom of your dreams, and you will together overcome any obstacle and temptation that tries to overtake you. That is the promise from God—the bride will be a loving wife and mother, and the groom will be a committed, loving husband and father. Both will be called blessed and live happily ever after in the sight of God.

The question is,

Is this promise worth the wait? Are you willing to wait and do what is right in the sight of God?

Becoming The Bride of Christ

For many, the ultimate goal in life is to find the man or woman of our dreams, or for that spouse of our dreams to find us. As much as we may wish for that to happen, it may and it may not. However, there is "The Perfect One" just waiting for us to accept him. For girls or women, He wants to be their bridegroom, not in a physical sense but in a spiritual sense. For boys or men, he wants to hold the most important place in their heart, be considered first and above all others. All human beings have a certain void in their hearts that only "The Perfect One" can fill.

In fact, the Bible does tell of another "Bride" and "Bridegroom," not referring to a woman and man as we might think. It even tells us the name of bride-groom, the price that was paid, and the terms of the contract. The Bible tells us about the Father of the Bridegroom, of the mansions His son is building and the marriage feast. This Bridegroom the Bible speaks of is Jesus, God's son, the Christ. He is the Anointed One, the Shekinah Glory of His Father, and His home is now in heaven where He is ruler and reigns with His father as King. His property is vast, and it is a kingdom that will last throughout all eternity.

The Bible also speaks of the Bride. She is the one who has accepted Him by faith as her Bridegroom, just as He has accepted her and is preparing her for the day she will come to Him. It is written that God the Father sent His Son, Jesus, about two thousand years ago to find His Bride. He came with the mohar of His life, because she was priceless, and He signed the ketubah with His blood, giving the matton of His Word and the Holy Spirit, promising that He will come back for her. He has gone back to His Father's house and now is preparing for the time He will take His Bride away. His Bride will be the one who has accepted Him, by faith, as her Bridegroom for all eternity.

If you agree to the terms of His Word, and if you accept Him by faith into your heart, it is as if you entered into the kiddushin and became His betrothed and are now awaiting His return. You will be separated by your faith unto Him alone and wear the veil of salvation.

There are gifts that He has given to His Bride to remember Him until He returns for her. Each time she partakes of the emblems at the communion table, she is to remember the sacrifice He made for her. When she drinks of the wine, she will remember the price He paid, with His precious blood, and will be remembering Him until the time when they will drink of it together when her redemption will be complete. When she partakes of the bread, it will remind her of the marriage supper and the celebration of her new eternal home, her "happily ever after."

While she waits, she prepares for His coming. He has left behind gifts for her, gifts to remind her of His love for her. He has given to her the contract of His Word and the anointing of the Holy Spirit. Wisdom of the Word will give her the understanding as the day approaches. This is given to her to prepare her to rule and reign as she will be forever His Queen. Her desire and love grows deeper for Him as the Holy Spirit reveals His heart to her and teaches her His ways.

He has also left for His Bride the precious gifts of pure essential oils, to anoint and be anointed, to remind her and carry on the authority she has been given as the wife of The Father's Son, Jesus, the Christ, and the Anointed One. The sweet-smelling fragrance of the sacrifice of her prayers and worship will remind her of the beauty of His Holiness in Spirit, soul and body. It will be the guarantee of the glory, power, love and covering of the Father's Son. It will bring her to a higher place of worship to her now Bridegroom, High Priest, and King. She will cherish these precious gifts as her very own as she eagerly awaits the lover of her soul, even as He is at the mansion of His Father, where He is preparing the room for His beautiful Bride to dwell with Him forever.

At any moment, the Father could tell His Son to go for His Bride. When He comes for His "Bride," who is actually all who believe, she, too, will be without spot or wrinkle because she has been washed in the water of baptism and immersed with the power of the Holy Spirit. When He comes for her, there will be a shout to awaken her at the midnight hour with the sound of the trumpet. There will be many suitors, and the wait might be long, but when love awakens, the Bride will know. With her heart prepared for that glorious day, with her oil lamp filled, she eagerly awaits the arrival of her beloved at the midnight hour to take her away.

When the mansion is complete, his Father will give the okay. Jesus, the Bridegroom, with a shout, will send forth his messengers, and, at the sound of the trump, his angels will be sent to escort his Bride to meet the Beloved. They will enter the bridal chamber to complete the nisu'in, and it is here that she will stand before Him and bare her heart and soul to Him. As He accepts her for His own, she will be anointed and adorned with the crown of His Glory in the covering of her new garments. She will finally drink of the cup of wine with Him for her redemption, and the covenant will now be complete. She will emerge to celebrate with the family of God at the marriage supper, but not before she casts her crown to Her King, her King of Glory.

This celebration with all believers will not last for seven days but for seven years, and after that time, He will take her to her new home in the New Jerusalem. In a New Heaven and a New

Earth, in the Kingdom of God, she will rule as queen and will reign with Him forever; indeed, there she will live happily ever after.

Will You Wait?

There is a man, a perfect man, who is wooing you to be His Bride. He is the Bridegroom, and His name is Jesus. His Father sees you as the perfect bride for His Son and has paid the price for you with His love and sacrifice. He stands at the door and knocks, and if you will open your heart, He will come in and be your bridegroom. It does not matter from which family you come. It does not matter what you have done or even if you have had other suitors. If you are now willing to forsake all others, make Him your own and wait, preparing for His coming, then His kingdom will also be yours, and forever His Queen you will be.

The choice is yours; He has given it to you.

The question is,

Is He worth the wait? Are you willing to wait and do what is right in the sight of God?

The Right of Refusal for the Bride and the Bridegroom

As with all contracts, there always is the right of refusal. Although the Father may arrange the bride for the bridegroom, she does have the right of refusal, and so does He. Her right of refusal could be that she has another offer, or her desire for Him just is not there. The Bridegroom will only accept the Bride who will cherish and love Him and who is willing to be Queen. This marriage will only be as good as the commitment that was made. As the gentleman He is, the Bridegroom will never force His love on an unwilling Bride, and He will leave her to her own heart's desire.

His right of refusal can be when He comes at the midnight hour to take her to their eternal home. If she was not where she promised she would be, or if she was not wise to be prepared for His coming, He will return to His Father's house without her, where the chamber door will forever be closed.

He Has Come to the Table, Will You Accept?

In this story, we see the beauty of the bride, and the love and care that was meant for her. Ancient customs and symbolisms of the Bible were put into place to have meaning and purpose for all of us. They were not only to fulfill our happily ever after here on earth, but also for all eternity. Since the beginning of time, the Father has made plans for you and has chosen YOU to live happily ever after with Him, His Son and the family of God for all eternity. The love and value God has placed on you is so much greater than the value that we have placed on those that we love.

Two thousand years ago, He sent His son for you. He has come with the bride price that has been paid with His blood, and drank of the cup of wine. He is waiting for you at the table to accept His offer. When you accept His offer, His gifts are ready for the taking and He will add on to His Father's house a mansion built just for you. When it is complete and He is ready to take you home, His Father, with a shout and the blast of the trumpet, will send His flaming angels to escort you home to Him.

He, with all those who believed and accepted Him as king, will meet you on your way to bring you back to the bridal chamber under the chuppah. Without spots and without wrinkles, you will be beautiful as you bare all to Him. He will cover you with His anointing, cover you with the new garments of His Glory, and He will crown you forever as Queen.

Being now complete, you will appear before the family of God, and the great celebration of the marriage supper will begin with a feast that will last for seven years. After the seven years, when all evil and temptations have been destroyed on the earth and all has been made perfect, you will reside in the New Heaven and New Earth. Then, in such a great kingdom, happily ever after you truly will be, not His bride now, but His Queen for all eternity.

The question now is,

Will you accept?

And the Spirit

and the Bride

say,

"Come!"

Revelation 22:17

Bibliography

Schauss, Hayim. *The Lifetime of a Jew.* New York: Union of American Hebrew Congregations, 1950

Ettinger, Annette. *Biblical Botanicals.* Hummelstown: The Ministries of Hegai, 2005

The Holy Bible, King James Version

About the Author

Donna Gallina and her husband Ron reside in Vineland, New Jersey. They have been in pastoral ministry for 15 years. Donna is a Certified Health Coach with certifications in Aromatherapy Research and Education for Raindrop. Donna and her husband have blended their passion for the Word of God with their desire for healthy living into their ministry, Creating Health, LLC.

Pastor Ron shares from the Word of God, and Donna flows in the prophetic gifts, sharing words of knowledge and songs during ministry presentations. They share unique combination of teaching the power and purpose of Scripture with anointing and prayer.

This biblical health journey began when Donna received a miraculous healing from God for her defective skeletal system

Donna's favorite book is The Bible, but she also enjoys reading about Jewish religious practices and customs, especially the use of essential oils. Actually, Donna's extensive personal experience with essential oils provided her with an excellent background for research when preparing this book. Her love for God, her interest in Jewish customs and her concern for today's American culture played a part, but it was the Lord's calling that prompted her to write this book in order to help restore the tradition of the marriage covenant. Donna gives all credit to the Lord. She prays that its concepts will bring a deeper understanding of ancient Jewish practices to her readers and that it will inspire them to consider the value of following Biblical examples in a society where so much has been lost.

To purchase the alabaster jar, essential oils, Biblical Botanicals or other merchandise, you may contact them through www.creatinghealth.us

To have a presentation For the Love of the Bride,
e-mail your request to thefragrantbride@aol.com